This Book Belongs To

_____

OUR BOOK RANGE

For more visit
www.grantpublishingltd.com

Book design and editing by Josephine Grant

40 Facts About Tanzania

Grant Publishing

Bite-sized facts and stunning photographs about the wonderful country that is Tanzania. A great choice to introduce your child to the world around them.

GRANT
PUBLISHING

Tanzania is
a country in the
continent of
Africa.

Tanzania is located on the Eastern part of Africa.

Tanzania is the largest country in East Africa.

Serengeti,
Tanzania

Tanzania is officially called The United Republic of Tanzania.

Ngorongoro, Tanzania

Tanzania borders Uganda, Kenya, Comoros, Malawi, Zambia, Burundi, Mozambique and DRC.

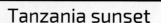

Tanzania sunset

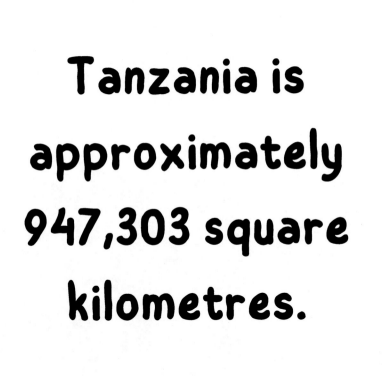

Tanzania is approximately 947,303 square kilometres.

Zanzibar, Tanzania

The capital city of Tanzania is Dodoma.

Dodoma, Tanzania

Dar es Salaam is the largest city in Tanzania.

Dar es Salaam, Tanzania

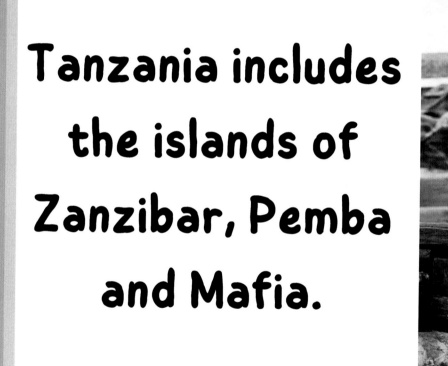

Tanzania includes the islands of Zanzibar, Pemba and Mafia.

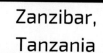

Zanzibar, Tanzania

Tanzania has a population of around 61 million people.

People from
Tanzania are
called
Tanzanian.

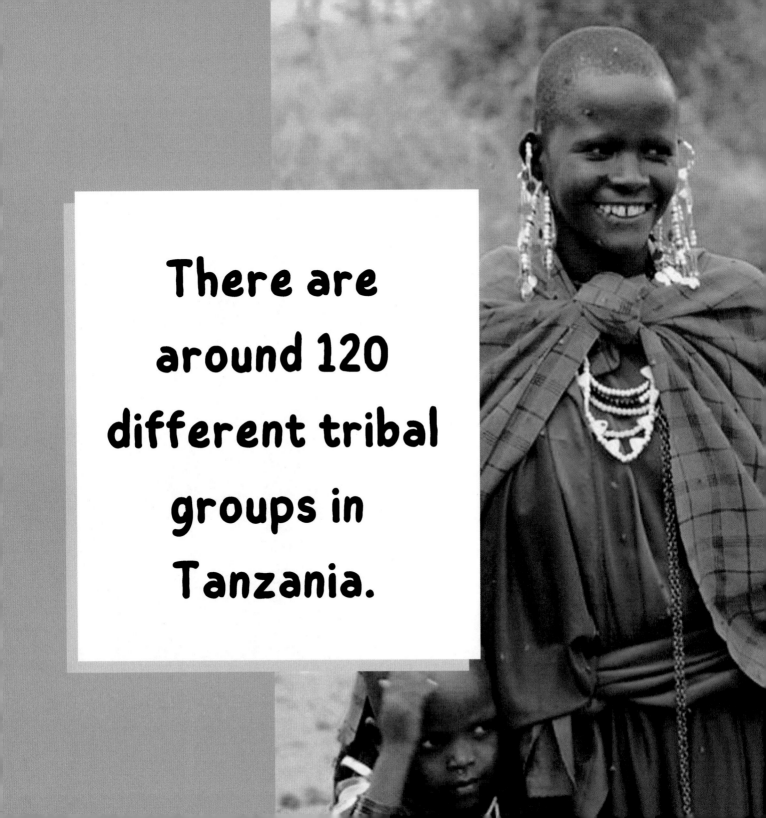

There are around 120 different tribal groups in Tanzania.

The largest tribal group in Tanzania is the Sakuma people.

The official languages of Tanzania are English and Swahili.

There are over 100 different languages spoken in Tanzania.

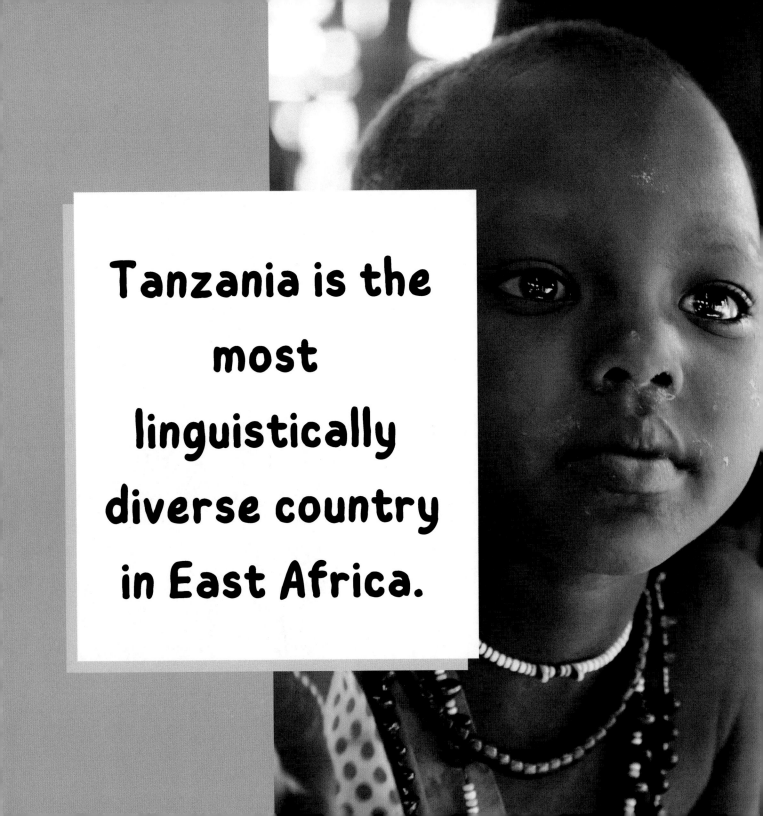

Tanzania is the most linguistically diverse country in East Africa.

The motto of Tanzania is "Uhuru na Umoja".

Zanzibar, Tanzania

The national anthem of Tanzania is "Mungu ibariki Afrika".

The national anthem is 'Udzima wa ya Masiwa'.

Mpanda, Tanzania

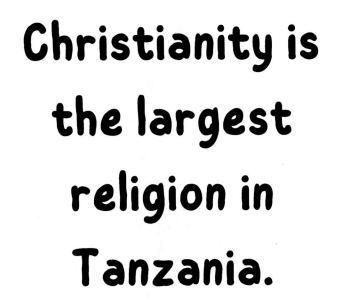

Christianity is the largest religion in Tanzania.

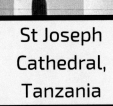

St Joseph
Cathedral,
Tanzania

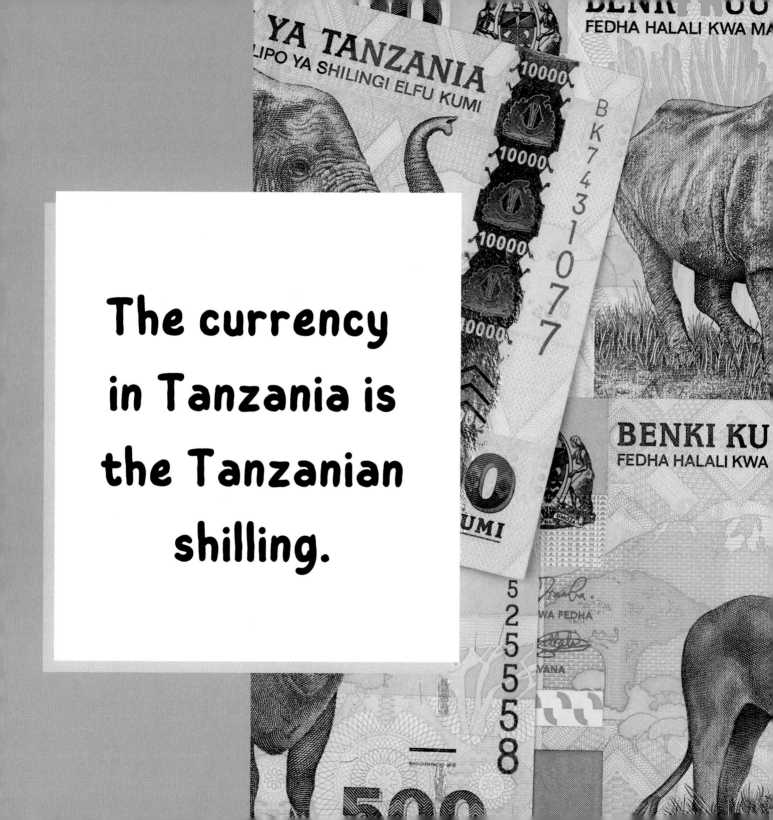

The currency in Tanzania is the Tanzanian shilling.

Tanzania gained independence from the United Kingdom on December 6th 1961.

Tanzania is a member of the Commonwealth.

Tanzania was once ruled by Germany.

Tanzania is known for its vast wilderness areas which includes the plains of Serengeti National Park.

Serengeti is a safari mecca populated by the big five game (lion, leopard, rhino, buffalo, elephant)

Nearly 30 per cent of Tanzania is national parks such as Tarangire national park.

There is a large variety of wildlife in Tanzania which includes zebras, giraffes and rhinos.

Tanzania contains around 20 per cent of Africa's warm blooded animal populace.

The Masai giraffe is Tanzania's national animal.

Tanzania has the largest lion population in the world.

Tanzania has two major rainfall periods.

Three of Africa's great lakes run through Tanzania; Lake Victoria, Lake Tanganyika and Lake Malawi.

Lake Victoria

Lake Tanganyika in Tanzania is the second largest lake in the world.

Lake Tanganyika

Tanzania is home to many beautiful waterfalls such as Kalambo and Materuni Falls.

Materuni Falls, Tanzania

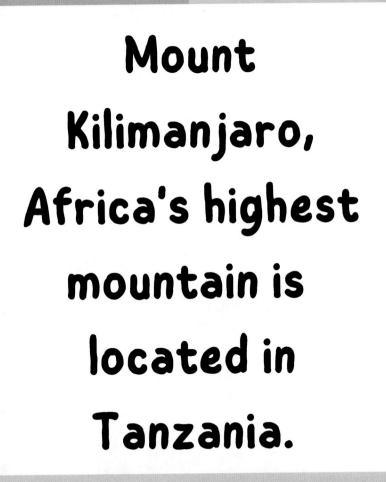

Mount Kilimanjaro, Africa's highest mountain is located in Tanzania.

Mount Kilimanjaro

Staple foods in Tanzania are beans, meat, cassava, ugali and small fish.

Ugali is the national dish of Tanzania.

Ugali

Tanzania is the world's only source of tanzanite, a semi-precious stone.

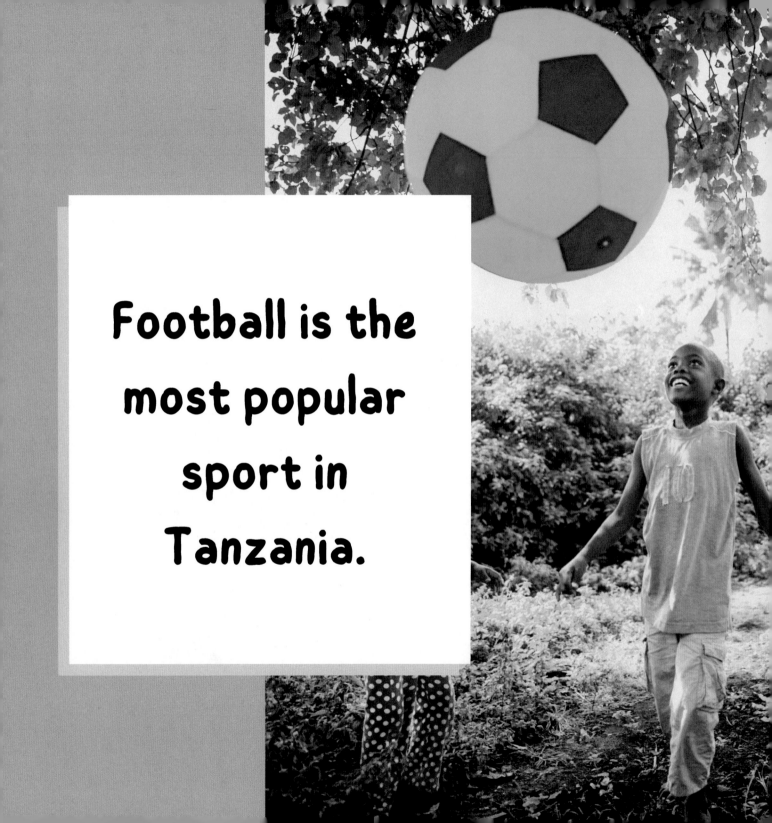

Football is the most popular sport in Tanzania.

WHAT WAS YOUR FAVOURITE FACT?

Made in the USA
Middletown, DE
11 August 2024

58924903R00027